Affirmations

1000+ Positive and Daily Affirmations for Wealth, Success, Money, Abundance, Health, Love and Positive Thinking

Contents

Part 1: Affirmations for Wealth

250 Positive Affirmations About Living in Abundance Now and Attracting Money

Introduction

You are what you think, said Earl Nightingale in his famous book "The Strangest Secret". You become what you think about most of the times. If a person feeds his mind with negative thoughts, he will experience life through a dark lens. Small things that shouldn't affect him will become bigger than they really are as the mind is focused on the worst instead of the best. A person living with mostly negative thoughts has a mind focused on problems, instead of opportunities. Now, do you want to know a sad truth? Most people live in a such a mind. And can you really blame them? Most of the media outlets certainly do not help us to achieve a blissful state of mind. Their mantra is "negative news sells" and thus they engage in fear mongering. And do you want to know another sad truth? It works darn well for them. The reason it works is because we humans are designed to survive and not to thrive. While it is good for our species that our brain has its default mode focused on survival, it doesn't guarantee personal success. If it did, we'd see more people flourishing both personally and financially.

Now the good thing for you is that you're already ahead of most people as you certainly are aware of the power of the mind. You probably already know that your mind is like a strong computer capable of incredibly impressive things. Your job is like that of a programmer's. You need to stay guard at the doors of your mind and feed it with empowering words.

This book can help you if you want to live in a state of abundance. Furthermore, by using the affirmations within this book, you'll hopefully be able to spot opportunities for creating wealth that you were unable to see before. To benefit the most from this book, it's recommended you pause and reuse an affirmation that you feel particularly resonates with you. Also, for affirmations to work effectively, you must put your heart into the ideas being presented. Leave the sceptic at the door and trust the process so you can reach your goals and dreams! Let's begin, shall we?

A Few Words About Using Affirmations Effectively

Firstly, state the affirmation in the present tense. Your goal is to feel as if you already have the things you want, no matter the outer circumstances. This will help you attract what you want in the present.

Secondly, your affirmations must only contain positive words. The reason to avoid negative words such as 'no', 'never' or 'not' is that your subconscious cannot process negative words. Instead, it removes the negative words so for example an affirmation stating, "I'm not poor" will become I'm poor" which is the opposite of what you want.

Thirdly, affirmations should be specific and deal with one goal at the time. You can have several affirmations about different topics but aim to keep the individual affirmation focused.

Fourthly, it's recommended to practice an affirmation at least 20 times thrice a day. Continue this practice until your mind completely accepts the affirmation as true. Once it does, repeat the affirmation on a continuous basis to reinforce the effect of that suggestion. Strive to make the daily use of affirmations a lifelong practice.

Keep these important ideas in mind and adhere to them when creating a personal affirmation. This will ensure you affirm the right suggestions and set you up for success.

Chapter 1 – 50 Gratitude Affirmations

"When you are grateful, fear disappears and abundance appears"

- Tony Robbins

Gratitude is the foundation for living in a state of abundance and without it, you won't find true fulfilment as your mind never appreciates the abundance you already have. Think about it, you live better than a king did just a couple of centuries ago. One could argue that you even life better than a king did only a couple of decades ago since you have such useful technology at your disposal. I among many other people also believe that gratitude will attract more good things into one's life, including wealth. So, when you go through these affirmations, aim to feel gratitude and express them as if you're the wealthiest person in the world. Speak them with confidence and use your body in a way that will create emotion. Remember that motion creates emotion so by using your body in a confident way, you'll benefit the most from these affirmations.

- I am grateful for living in the 21th century.
- I am so thankful for all the money that I have.
- I feel appreciation for the things money allows me to buy.
- I love life and I'm so grateful to be a part of it.
- I know that life is a gift.
- While I inhale, I take full pleasure of the air that energizes my body and mind.
- I am so grateful for the opportunities life has given me.
- I'm so grateful for the opportunities life is continuing to give me.
- I feel gratitude towards people for I know that they can help me achieve my dreams.
- I am so grateful for who I am since I know that I can create magnificent things.
- I am grateful for being in control.
- I feel grateful for the people in my life.
- I am grateful for the opportunities to come.

- I was given the gift of life and the chance to make whatever I want of it, and for that I am grateful.

- I am grateful for all the resources that I have and those that are to come.

- I am grateful for my resourcefulness and my ability to find solutions.

- I see the good in events and people.

- I know that the chances of me being born were very low and I am so grateful for beating the odds.

- Gratitude is my antidote to fear and anger. I am now in control of my emotions.

- I am so grateful for my ability to produce.

- Every day, I am living life to the fullest as a thanks to God for giving me the gift of life.

- I am so grateful for my prosperous future.

- I am grateful for my health, wealth, love and happiness.

- An abundance of money is flowing to me right now and for that I am grateful.

- I am so grateful that people treat me with respect and care for my well-being.

- I am so grateful for having all my needs meet.

- I give thanks to the Universe for allowing me to live my dreams.

- I am the master of my life and for that, I am grateful.

- I am so grateful for being able to use the wonderful things that others have created.

- I am grateful for all the money ideas that come to me.

- I know that one only needs to be right one time to become financially prosperous and I am grateful that it's my turn now.

- I am grateful for I know that successful people want to help me, be it via books, videos or in person.

- I am grateful for the abundance of choices I've been given.

- I know that freedom is uncertain for some people in other parts of the world, that's why I appreciate that I've been born here.

- I am grateful for money.

- I am free to live life on my own terms, and for that I am grateful.

- I am grateful for the plenty of opportunities to create an abundance of money.

- I know that my mind can create incredible things and for that, I am grateful.

- I am so grateful for having multiple sources of income.

- I am so grateful that money comes to me in avalanches of abundance from unexpected sources on a continuous basis.

- I love all the events money can allow me to experience.

- I am grateful for my incredible ability to solve problems and bring immense value to the market place.

- I am grateful for my commitment to live in abundance.

- I know that I can feel the feeling of abundance whenever I want, and for that I am so grateful.

- I hereby give thanks to the Universe for all the prosperity I experience.

- Money flows effortlessly to me and for that, I am grateful.

- Gratitude is a gift of life and I experience it daily.

- Abundance is a natural state for me and I love it.

- I live better than hundreds of kings before me and for that, I am grateful.

- I am so grateful that money flows with ease into my bank account.

Chapter 2 – 50 Abundance Affirmations

"When you focus on being a blessing, God makes sure that you are always blessed in abundance."
- Joel Osteen

To live a life of true abundance, we first must make a conscious decision to live in a beautiful state no matter what. Life does not happen to us, it happens for us and with that knowledge in mind, we can trust that the Universe is taking care of us and guiding us to the person we want to be as well as our desired place. So trust the process and choose to relax by breathing deeply whenever challenges arise. They are put in place to make you who God has intended you to be.

- Gods wealth is circulating in my life.

- I hereby chose to live in a beautiful state.

- The Universe has my best interest at heart.

- I experience avalanches of abundance and all my needs are met instantaneously.

- Abundance is something we tune in to.

- I choose to live in abundance in every moment of everyday for the rest of my life.

- I know that I am being guided to my true self.

- I live in financial abundance.

- I know that my needs are always met and that answers are given to me.

- Everyday in every way, I am becoming more and more abundant.

- The Universe takes good care of me as I always have what I need.

- My life is full of all the material things I need.

- My life is filled with joy and love.

- Money flows to me in abundance.

- I have everything in abundance.

- Prosperity overflows in my life.

- My thoughts are always about prosperity and abundance.

- My actions lead to prosperity and abundance.

- I hereby focus on prosperity and abundance and thereby attract it into my life.

- Abundance and prosperity is within me as well as around me.

- I hereby allow all great things to come into my life.

- I enjoy the good things that flows into my life.

- I create prosperity easily and effortlessly.

- I feel passionate about prosperity and thus it comes to me naturally.

- I love abundance and I naturally attract it.

- The whole Universe is conspiring to make me abundant and prosperous.

- I let go of any resistance to abundance and prosperity and it comes to me naturally.

- I am grateful for the prosperity and abundance in my life.

- I am open and receptive to all the prosperity life is now willing to give me.

- I am surrounded by prosperity.

- I deserve to be wealthy.

- My visions are becoming a reality.

- Thank you Universe for all that you've given me.

- I am a money magnet.

- Prosperity is naturally drawn to me.

- I am always using abundance thinking.

- I am worthy of becoming financially prosperous.

- I am one with the energy of abundance.

- I use money to better my life as well as the lives of others.

- I am the master of money

- Money is my servant.

- I can handle large sums of money.

- I enjoy having an abundance of money.

- I am at peace with large sums of money flowing to me.

- Money leads to opportunities and experiences.

- An abundance of money creates positive impact in my life.

- It's my birthright to live in a state of abundance.

- The Universe is guiding me to more prosperity right now.

- Money is coming to me in large quantities and I am ready for it.

- People want me to live in abundance and I know I deserve it.

Chapter 3 – 50 Affirmations about Attracting Money

"Thoughts become things. If you see it in your mind, you will hold it in your hand."

— Bob Proctor, You Were Born Rich

Money tends to come to those who have a prosperity mindset. The gratitude and abundance affirmations that we've gone through in previous chapters should have lifted up your invisible money magnet so you can start attracting an abundance of wealth into your life. The following are 50 affirmations about attracting money.

- I'm filled with joy and gratitude and I love that more and more money is flowing to me continuously.

- Money is flowing to me in avalanches of abundance from unexpected sources.

- Money is coming to me faster and faster.

- I deserve prosperity and to have an abundance of money in my bank account.

- All my dreams, goals and desires are met instantaneously.

- The Universe is on my side and it is guiding me towards wealth.

- The Universe is guiding wealth towards me.

- I love money and all that it can buy.

- I feel grateful that I increase my net worth substantially every year.

- Money flows to me with ease.

- Ideas to make more money is coming to me often.

- I feel good about money.

- I can do good things with money.

- I am worthy of prosperity and having an abundance of money.

- I release all my negative beliefs about money and allow for financial abundance to enter.

- Money is always close to me.

- Opportunities to make more money come to me effortlessly.

- I give value and money loves me for it.

- I attract money with ease and I now have more wealth than I ever dreamed possible.

- I am wealthy, and I feel incredibly good about it.

- I have a great relationship with money.

- I am gracious for all the money that I have.

- Every day and in every way, I am attracting more money into my life.

- Being wealthy feels fantastic.

- I attract money effortlessly.

- I now allow for money to flow freely into my life.

- I am a money magnet and money will always be attracted to me.

- I am now relaxing into greater prosperity.

- I release all opposition to money.

- I deserve to have a lot of money in my bank account.

- Ideas of making money is freely entering my life.

- Abundance is all around me and I feel so gracious about it.

- Being wealthy is my natural state.

- The Universe is helping me to attract money into my life right now.

- I am prosperous, and I appreciate all the good things in my life.

- I am affluent.

- It feels phenomenal to have a lot of money in my bank account.

- I love money and money loves me.

- It's very easy for me to make more money.

- I am a natural born money maker.

- I am willing and ready to receive more money now.

- My income increases substantially each year.

- I happily receive money with ease.

- The Universe keeps giving me more and more money.

- Attracting money is easy for me.

- Money is good and with it I can help other people better their life.

- Financial success is my birth right.

- An avalanche of money is transporting itself to me.

- I feel good about receiving large quantities of money.

- Thank you Universe for allowing me to live in prosperity.

Chapter 4 – 100 Success and Wealth Affirmations

"Your positive action combined with positive thinking results in success"

- Shiv Khera

In this chapter, we'll go through affirmations you can use to get a successful mind. What is a successful mind? Well it's a mind that contains positive and empowering beliefs about success regarding all aspects of life. It has been said that people fear success more than failure, and with that mindset, it is hard to achieve anything extraordinary. The affirmations below will not only help you overcome any subconscious blocks that might be holding you back from living your dreams, but they will also prime your mind to spot any wealth creating opportunities and more importantly; encourage you to act on them.

- My beliefs shape my reality.

- I realize that I'm the creator of my life.

- I decide to make my life a masterpiece.

- I know that if I believe it I can see it.

- I have always been destined to become wealthy.

- I find a lot of opportunities for creating prosperity and abundance.

- I give and receive.

- I live by the words "let go and grow". That's why I find it easy to forgive myself and others.

- I'm grateful for the lessons my past has given me.

- I'm a great giver; I'm also a great receiver.

- I understand that my abundance of money can make the world a better place.

- The universe responds to my mindset of abundance by giving me more prosperity.

- I define my dream and feel gratitude for its realization.

- I visualize living my dream every day.

- I send out good vibrations about money.

- I'm abundant in every way.

- I'm grateful for all the money that I have. I'm grateful for all the prosperity that I receive.

- I'm grateful for the present moment and focus on the beauty of life.

- I pay myself first and make my money multiply.

- I have a millionaire mind and I now understand the principles behind wealth.

- I love the freedom that money gives me.

- I'm a multi-millionaire.

- I choose to be me and free.

- There is an infinite amount of opportunities for creating wealth in the world.

- I see opportunities for creating wealth and act on them.

- My motto is act and adapt.

- The answers always seem to come to me.

- I have an attitude of gratitude.

- I deserve to become wealthy.

- I deserve to have the best in life.

- I'm a wonderful person with patience.

- I trust the universe to guide me to my true calling in life. Knowing this I get a feeling of calmness.

- I know that I'm becoming the best I can possibly be.

- I feel connected to prosperity.

- I love money and realize all the great things it can do.

- I'm at one with a tremendous amount of money.

- Money loves me and therefore it will keep flowing to me.

- I use my income wisely and always have a big surplus of money at the end of the month.

- I truly love the feeling of being wealthy. I enjoy the freedom it gives me.

- It is easy for me to understand how money works.

- I choose to think in ways that support me in my happiness and success.

- I'm an exceptional manager of money.

- I realize that success in anything leaves clues.

- I follow the formula of people who have created a fortune.

- I create a lot value for others.

- I'm a valuable person.

- My life is full of abundance.

- I know about the 80 20 rule which states that 80 % of the effects come from 20 % of the causes.

- 20 % of my activities produce 80 % of the results.

- I choose to focus on the most important things in my life.

- I choose to become wealthy.

- I make my money multiply by investing them wisely.

- I pay myself first. 10 % of my income works for me.

- Money works for me.

- I increase my ability to earn by setting concrete goals and work to achieve them.

- By implementing the 80 20 rule in my life I increase my productivity and profitability.

- I focus on the most important areas in my life and eliminate, delegate or automate the rest.

- Time is on my side now.

- Everyday I'm getting better, smarter and more skillful.

- I believe that other people want me to be successful and are happily helping me towards my dream.

- I know how to handle people.

- I smile often and remember the other person's name.

- I give sincere appreciation and focus on the other person.

- I make people feel important.

- I praise improvement and call attention to people's mistakes indirectly. I make fault seem easy to correct.

- I'm a great leader and people are happy about doing what I suggest.

- I'm a good listener who encourages the other person to talk about him or herself.

- I try honestly to see things from the other persons view.

- I cooperate with others; whose minds work in perfect harmony for the attainment of a common definite objective.

- I have a purpose and a plan.

- I'm courageous and understand that courage is not the absence of fear but rather the willingness to act in spite of it.

- I have self discipline and full control over my thoughts and emotion.

- I do the most important things first.

- I'm organized and remember the 80 20 rule.

- I expect the best in life. I know about the magic of thinking big.

- I always expect to win.

- I'm a confident person who takes action.

- I'm decisive and know what I want.

- I'm committed to my success.

- I know that where attention goes energy flows.

- I see opportunities and act on them.

- I write down my goals and program my subconscious mind for success.

- I will persist until I succeed.

- I only pray for guidance and I realize that I'm going to be tested.

- I get stronger by challenges.

- I live everyday as if it was my last.

- I realize that life is a gift.

- I'm grateful for being alive.

- I understand that being born is a miracle and I'm very grateful for it.

- I'm more than I seem to be and all the powers of the universe are within me.

- I feel abundance and love.

- I trust myself; my gut feeling knows the truth.

- I harness my intuition and know that people might be like me, but that I'm unique.

- My DNA and the way my brain is configured is completely unique.

- I love myself and understand that I'm the only one who can be me.

- I focus on my inclinations and the things I'm good at.

- I develop my talents and abilities.

- I focus on adding value.

- The world will be a better place because I was here.

- I'm a valuable person who takes responsibility.

Conclusion

My goal with this book was to leave you feeling empowered. I hope the affirmations herein has equipped you with the right mindset to attract more wealth into your life.

Remember what Tony Robbins said: *When you are grateful, fear disappears and abundance appears*. There's always something to feel grateful for no matter what so don't limit your gratefulness to only big events. Feel gratitude towards the air your breathing, the food you've got access to or the water you're drinking. Gratitude is the key to inviting more great things into your life and ultimately living a life of abundance.

Lastly, I would invite you to consider the power of habits. What I want said with this is that you can leave this book now and never return to it, and you will have benefited from it. But if you come back to this book on a regular basis, you will integrate the changes on a much deeper level and that will lead to a more positive outcome in the long run.

I wish you all the best and I sincerely hope you'll enjoy life to the fullest!

If you enjoyed this first part of on Affirmations for Wealth, can you please leave a review for the individual book on Amazon?

Thanks for your support!

Part 2: Positive Affirmations

250 Daily Affirmations About Attracting Love, Making Money, Healthy Living, and Finding True Happiness

Introduction

In his book *Think and Grow Rich* the author Napoleon Hill states the following: "You are the master of your destiny. You can influence, direct and control your own environment. You can make your life what you want it to be."

This is what this book is about. It's a guide to help you control your destiny by using powerful affirmations that will focus your mind on what you want. These affirmations will work as a compass, always helping you to shift your focus to where it needs to be if you want to reach a certain destination. The certain destination this book is aiming to lead you towards is an abundance of health, wealth, love and happiness.

Before you start, remember the following: Be joyful now by learning to enjoy every minute of your life. Stop waiting for something outside of your own being to make you happy "someday" in the distant future. Contemplate on the preciousness of the time you got left, be it at work, or with your family. Enjoy every minute it of it as it shall never return.

Chapter 1 – 50 Money Affirmations

"Whoever said money can't buy happiness simply didn't know where to go shopping."

- Bo Derek

A lot of people have stated that money can't buy happiness. However, a study from Princeton University's Woodrow Wilson School says that it does indeed buy happiness if the person's income is below $75 000. Over that amount, there aren't any significant levels of increased happiness. Now, this does not mean that all people who make over $75 000 per year doesn't feel a significant increase in happiness, I'm confident that some do, just as there are people in third-world countries who are much happier than some billionaires. This study can only work as a general rule of thumb.

Leaving the discussion behind, I think we can agree that money is important, and that more money wouldn't hurt. However, a lot of people have unconscious associations to money that block them from attracting a great amount of it. Some of these limited beliefs might include nonsensical sayings such as:

1. Money is the root of all evil.

2. Money can't buy happiness.

3. Money is not everything.

4. People can make a lot of money, but they do it at the expense of their family.

5. It's selfish to have a lot of money.

You've probably heard at least one of these ridiculous statements before. Let's break each of these wacky sayings down, shall we?

Nr 1: *Money is the root of all evil.* Money is simply a means of exchange. Do you prefer we go back to barter? Finding someone who will want to change your apple for a pen will be both frustrating and time consuming. Money is neither good or bad. Yes indeed, you can do both good and bad things with money but stating that money itself is evil is just ludicrous. Think about all the good things people have done with money, all the lives they have saved. Think about all the people with money who have created companies in which people can work and earn a living. Think about all the good things you can do with money and all the lives you can better. If you think this limiting belief is holding you back from living in financial abundance, consider using the following affirmation: *Money is neutral and a resource to do good in my life.*

Nr 2: *Money can't buy happiness.* As we've already the mentioned before, there are studies showing that money can increase one's happiness up to a certain point and perhaps even beyond. Even if the statement "money can't buy happiness" was true (which it's not), money can buy time. And more time, can surely make one happier. For example, if you have a lot of money, you can hire other people to do chores that you don't particularly enjoy doing. Also think about all the experiences that money can buy. Whenever we are focused on the negative, we need to stop and ask ourselves; "what are the opportunities?" If you want an affirmation that will absolutely turn this limiting belief into the small ball of dust it really is, consider the following one:

I love money as it can buy me both experiences and time with my loved ones.

Nr 3: *Money is not everything.* Of course it's not everything Dum-Dum, but you need it don't you? Or how do you get food on the table and a roof over your head? Let's follow the advice, "don't argue with a foolish argument", regarding this one and just move on to the next one, shall we?

Nr 4: *People can make a lot of money, but they do it at the expense of their family.* Some individuals may prioritize work over spending time with their family. However, this does not make the statement an absolute truth. People seldom get rich by hard work alone. People acquire great wealth by doing the right things. Such things include making their money work for them by making smart investments or leveraging other people's time and money. To crush this limiting belief, start searching for people who are making a lot of money who work less than the average worker. I'm sure you will come across a lot of people who have found a way to use leverage to make a lot of money, perhaps even in an automated way. Also, consider the fact that the average person in America is watching around 5 hours of television per day. Surely there doesn't seem to be a shortage of time to spend with loved ones if one prioritizes differently? Here's an affirmation to let you overcome this limiting belief: *With more money, I can choose to spend more time with my family if I want to.*

Nr 5: *It's selfish to have a lot of money.* As mentioned before, money is simply a means of exchange. In other words, you change your money for something you want, or vise versa. This means that you must have provided something of perceived value to someone else to receive that money. Again, providing value doesn't have to be linked with your time. Investors can for example provide value by letting other people provide value with the help of their money. Either way, acquiring money is neither a selfish or unselfish act, it's simply an exchange of value. If you struggle with this limiting belief, consider replacing it by using the following affirmations: *The money I've earned reflects the value I've created for others.*

Hopefully this list, has helped you tackle the most disturbing false beliefs about money. If you think you have more, don't worry, the 50 money affirmations soon to come will surely help you overcome most of the silly associations that people tend to drop senselessly in to our mind as we get older. As Jim Rohn said, we must stay guard at the door of our mind every day!

Now, as you may have heard before; you can give a man a fish to feed him for a day or you can teach him how to fish so he can feed himself for a lifetime. I'll aim to do both; so here's two noteworthy ideas for you to consider when overcoming any limiting beliefs, be it regarding money, love, health or happiness. First, ask yourself this one simple question: Is this belief an absolute truth for me as an individual or can I find people or circumstances that proves that the opposite can also be true? Secondly, as you might have already noted, I've used rather harsh adjectives to describe some of these limiting beliefs. The reason for this is because I want to break a pattern and the easiest way to do that is by strong emotion or doing something unexpected. You can also add a voice to the limiting belief that is impossible for you to take seriously (for example, a voice from a South Park character). Imagine this voice combined with a face you can't take seriously and then visualize how this face is blowing up as a balloon and becoming smaller and smaller as it's flying away to some distant corner. You can also write down the limiting belief, then scrunch the paper and throw it in a garbage can. Personally, I like the voice method the best, but you choose whichever method or methods that works best for you.

Are you ready to start with the affirmations? Okay, here we go!

1. I'm so grateful for living in prosperity.

2. Every day, in every way, I'm attracting more and more money into my life.

3. I live in abundance now.

4. Money comes to me with ease.

5. I see many opportunities for creating wealth.

6. I give and receive with ease.

7. I feel gratitude for all the money that I have.

8. I'm a great giver; I'm also an exceptional receiver.

9. By being wealthy and having a lot of money, I can make the world a better place.

10. It feels fantastic to have a lot of money.

11. The universe responds to my prosperity mindset by giving me more opportunities to make money with ease.

12. I visualize being wealthy every day and I send out good vibrations about money.

13. I'm a money magnet that attracts money from all types of places.

14. I am abundant every day, in every way.

15. I'm gracious for all the prosperity I receive.

16. I pay myself first and my money multiplies.

17. An avalanche of money is now entering my life.

18. Making money is easy for me.

19. I constantly find and come up with new ways to make more money with ease.

20. Money is one important part of my life and I give it the time and attention it deserves.

21. Money allows me to help more people.

22. Money allows me to spend more time with my loved ones.

23. Money allows me to have more wonderful experiences.

24. Having more money is a good thing for me.

25. I love money and all the wonderful things it can do.

26. I love the freedom that money gives me.

27. I deserve to be wealthy and to live in abundance.

28. I attract money from all kinds of unexpected sources.

29. I continuously have a big surplus of money at the end of every month.

30. I am attracted to money and money is attracted to me.

31. I continuously learn from other people who live in financial abundance be it via books, videos, audio or in person.

32. My actions create a lot of value for others.

33. I am a person of great value.

34. I make my money work for me.

35. My money brings me more money.

36. I am a great money manager.

37. I see more and more great opportunities for creating wealth.

38. I am a multi-millionaire.

39. I am so grateful for ability to make a lot of money.

40. I am at one with a tremendous amount of money in my bank account.

41. My financial reality is in my control alone.

42. Money is my servant.

43. I have everything I need to create financial abundance.

44. There is enough money to create prosperity.

45. Being rich is easy.

46. I always have access to a lot of money.

47. I am worthy of being affluent.

48. I enjoy making money.

49. I enjoy having multiple streams of passive income.

50. I trust that the Universe always meets my needs.

Chapter 2 – 50 Love Affirmations

"Give and it will be given to you in good measure, pressed down and overflowing, they shall cast into your lap. For with what measure you measure it will be measured to you."

Luke 6:38

The best way to receive love, it to first give love. And the best way to be surrounded by loving people, it to first become a loving person. Why choose love instead of hate? Well, hate is too big of a burden to bear as Martin Luther King, Jr. put it. Love is powerful as it has the power to turn an enemy into a friend. But to express true love towards anyone else in your life, you must first love the most important person in your life which is you! You are incredibly complex, and there's no one with the exact same DNA and brain configuration as you. You have talents, abilities and inclinations that are unique to you and the best way to serve the world and people around you is use them in a positive way. So, love yourself for who you are, and you'll find that loving others will become second nature. Here are 50 affirmations about loving yourself, loving others and loving the world we live in.

1. I love the world and all its beauty.

2. God's love is circulating in my life as well as flows to me in avalanches of abundance.

3. I understand that I'm the only one who can be me and that I was made this way for a reason.

4. The world will be a better place because I was here.

5. I choose love, forgiveness and kindness.

6. I love myself and all the goods deeds I have made and will make.

7. I see loving eyes all around me.

8. I deserve to experience love.

9. I get love in abundance.

10. I give love and I receive love.

11. Every day and in every way, I'm choosing to look at life through a lens of love.

12. My life is now full of love as I have attracted the most loving person into my life.

13. I have the perfect partner and our love is incredibly strong.

14. I am a wonderful, trustworthy and understanding person.

15. I attract wonderful, trustworthy and understanding people into my life.

16. I forgive myself and others.

17. I do small things for others to show my love for them.

18. I radiate true love to my partner.

19. My partner radiates true love to me.

20. I give love freely and effortlessly.

21. I am open to receive love from the Universe.

22. I am open to receive love from other people.

23. I am an exceptional giver, and I'm also an exceptional receiver.

24. I am surrounded by other people who love and care for me.

25. I live in a loving and caring Universe.

26. I support my friends and family.

27. I attract relationships that are of pure and unconditional love.

28. I look at the good in life, and I see love all around me.

29. I am so happy and peaceful now that I've found the love within me.

30. I live in a romantic relationship with the partner of my dreams.

31. I love my healthy body.

32. I love my brain and all its abilities.

33. I find it easy to admire others and show appreciation.

34. I am super confident and other people are very attracted to my confidence.

35. I am being guided by a loving universe.

36. Love is my birthright and always find opportunities to experience love.

37. I am so grateful for having the most wonderful and loving partner in my life.

38. I acknowledge the good in others and make fault seem easy to correct.

39. I am an excellent and loving leader and others are naturally attracted to my being.

40. My mind, heart and soul work in perfect harmony to create love all the time.

41. My efforts are being supported by a loving Universe.

42. I only need my own approval.

43. I trust myself and my ability to make the right choices.

44. I trust my gut feeling and intuition to guide me to an ever-loving destination.

45. I accept others as they are and in turn the accept me for who I am.

46. My mind contains loving thoughts about myself and others.

47. I attract love easily and effortlessly.

48. I am worthy of feeling self-love and a love for others.

49. I am love.

50. I now live in a beautiful state filled with abundance and love.

Chapter 3 – 50 Affirmations about Health

"Calm mind brings inner strength and self-confidence so that's very important for good health."

- Dalai Lama

Kris Karr is a cancer survivor who went on to become a best-selling author. She has stated that if you don't think sadness, depression or anxiety can affect your physical health, then you should think again because all these emotions trigger chemical reactions in your body. Chemical reactions that can lead to inflammation and a weakened immune system. She definitely has a point as there is growing evidence linking emotions to physical function.

But what creates emotion? The answer is our thoughts, and motion. Here's how it works: Let's say your car is not starting, in that moment, you have two choices. You can say; why is this happening to me and create a victim mentality around it. In such a case, your thoughts will spark a certain kind of motion in your body. You may frown your face, slump your shoulders and begin to breath shallower. If you on the other hand react with a stoic mindset, and remind yourself that you can't control what happened, you can only control your response, then you might react differently. You may begin by taking a deep breath and then shift your mind from the event towards things to be grateful for. For example, you could say; well I'm so grateful that I'm home and that this didn't occur when I was driving or when I was stranded in a freezing cold environment. There's always something to be grateful for, and you're doing this for one main reason; you can't be grateful and angry at the same time. And as we've discussed, you don't want to feel anger as that can cause ill health because anger elicits certain chemical reactions.

So in conclusion, when things don't go as planned, think about the way you react with your body. Breath deeply, stand in a superhero stance, and think about things you are grateful for. Now you have a much better chance of solving the challenge quickly and with ease while maintaining your physical health.

Here are 50 affirmations not only about maintaining your health, but also about improving it.

1. I am full of energy and full of life.
2. I control my state at all times.
3. I am happy and always in control of how I feel.

4. I decide to be feel gratitude and joy right now.

5. I am more than I seem to be, and all the powers of the Universe are within me.

6. My reason for eating is to fuel my body.

7. Being healthy is better than any taste in the world.

8. My healthy thoughts create my healthy body.

9. My body is my temple.

10. I am worthy of being healthy.

11. My daily habits are leading me to become healthier and healthier.

12. I choose to eat healthy because the food I eat is construction material for my body.

13. I eat nutritious foods that give me energy.

14. It's okay for me to eat for enjoyment or social reason if I do it responsibly and stay within my own rules that I've set in advance.

15. I get plenty of energizing sleep.

16. I make healthy choices and respect the body I've been given.

17. The water I drink cleanse my body and give me clarity of mind.

18. I love being healthy and it feels wonderful.

19. I take deep breaths every day and remind myself that air is a gift.

20. I am in control of my own health.

21. Every cell in my body embodies the spirit of health.

22. I love myself and the body I've been given.

23. Everyday and in every way, I am becoming more and more healthy.

24. I feel great and I radiate joy and gratitude.

25. I am vigorous and full of vitality.

26. I now demand my body to release all ill feelings about events or people.

27. I now forgive myself as well as other people.

28. I am a creator, I create my future and decide my own health.

29. I deserve to live a life filled with energy and joy.

30. I honor my body and I am surrounded by people who want me to be healthy.

31. I trust the signals my body sends me.

32. I am so grateful to be alive and to feel good.

33. My thoughts are supporting my body to become healthier and healthier.

34. I give my body what it needs.

35. I love every cell of this body that I have.

36. I am always healing rapidly, and I constantly feel wonderful.

37. I fill my mind with positive thoughts.

38. I use my body in a way that creates positive emotions.

39. I smile often and stand up straight.

40. I release the past and relish the present moment.

41. The Universe is conspiring to keep me healthy.

42. I relax my jaw and keep my teeth separated slightly.

43. I relax my body often and let my body rest when it needs to.

44. I do things that are good for my body.

45. I feel incredibly healthy and I love it.

46. I am strong and feel good about myself.

47. I am at peace with my health.

48. My mind is brilliant, and my soul is tranquil.

49. I always sleep in peace and wake up with incredible joy.

50. I love exercising and eating healthy foods.

Chapter 4 – 100 Positive Affirmations about Happiness, Joy, Confidence and Gratitude

"Happiness is not something ready made. It comes from your own actions."

- Dalai Lama

The first step to becoming happy is to change one's thoughts. Affirmations is great for this as it can replace a limiting or false belief with a more empowering one. Now, it's important to note that you shouldn't try to force negative thoughts to disappear. Resistance is not the key here. Instead, become aware of the thought, and accept it without putting any judgement on it. By just being aware and present, you should find that the thought will slowly back away just as an uninvited guest would if he realized he had gone to the wrong party.

A lot of people are looking for happiness in big things or events when in fact, there's often more power in extracting happiness from common things and experiences. So don't wait to be happy as you can choose to be it right here and now. Also, remember that your physiology is a very important piece to feeling happy. You aren't going to feel much happiness if you have your head down and a frown on your face. If you on the other hand, lift your head up, straighten your back and put a big smile on your face, then you're going to feel a lot better and you'll find it easier to think more positive. When speaking the affirmations in the chapter, remember to use your body in a confident way.

1. Every day, and in every way, I'm experiencing more and more joy in my life.

2. Happiness is my natural state.

3. I deserve to be happy.

4. By being happy, I help others to become happy.

5. I am so grateful for the joyful feeling that follows me everywhere.

6. I spread happiness to others and absorb happiness from others.

7. I am so happy and grateful now that my outlook on life is positive.

8. Being happy is easy for me.

9. I am grateful for every moment of every day for I know it shall never return.

10. My future is bright, and I am so thankful for it.

11. I think uplifting thoughts.

12. Life is easy for me.

13. I am grateful for the air I'm breathing, the water I got access to and the food in my fridge.

14. I always have what I need and for that, I'm grateful.

15. I start everyday in a state of happiness and joy.

16. I am a joyful giver and a happy receiver of good things in my life.

17. I am meant to be here in this world and fulfil a purpose.

18. The world will be a better and happier place because I was here.

19. I am an unstoppable force for good.

20. I trust myself, my inner wisdom knows the truth.

21. I forgive myself and others for all the mistakes made.

22. I breathe in happiness with every breath I take.

23. This day brings me happiness.

24. I wake up feeling grateful for life.

25. Today is my day to shine light on the world.

26. Everything always works out for the best for me.

27. I trust the Universe to guide me to my true calling in life.

28. I am so happy and grateful now that I get to live my dream.

29. I am always improving and learning new things.

30. I am present and feel joy in this moment.

31. I can transform any negative into a positive.

32. I am a positive person with incredible gifts to give to the world.

33. I am the creator of my day, my weeks, my months and my years.

34. I decide to make my life a masterpiece worth remembering.

35. I feel alive and the world around me feels fresh and new.

36. I breathe deeply and connect with my inner being.

37. Thank you, thank you, thank you.

38. Life is wonderful, and I love living.

39. There are endless opportunities to experience joy and happiness every day.

40. I transform obstacles into opportunities.

41. I am eternally grateful for the abundance in my life.

42. I make a conscious decision to be happy.

43. My life is overflowing with happiness and joy.

44. I am so grateful that I get to live another day.

45. The world is a beautiful place.

46. I deserve whatever great comes my way today.

47. I am a great receiver of wonderful things and experiences.

48. I am a magnet that always attract positive things and events.

49. I believe in myself.

50. I am a confident person with a positive mindset.

51. I always have more than enough to be happy.

52. I live an uplifting life and I always attract positive things into it.

53. Time is my most valuable asset; I therefore spend it in the best way possible.

54. I always hold the power to decide what I wish to do with my life.

55. I love life and life loves me.

56. The Universe is guiding me towards my higher purpose in life.

57. I am in full control of my thoughts and emotions.

58. I allow myself to have fun and enjoy life.

59. I am at peace with a tremendous amount of happiness and joy.

60. I trust that what's happening is happening for the greater good.

61. I create a vision for my life and a plan to achieve it.

62. I trust my ability to find solutions.

63. The Universe is always looking out for me.

64. Today, I am feeling confident and strong.

65. This day is another well written page in my life's book.

66. I only compare myself to my highest self.

67. I am grounded and secure in my being.

68. I surround myself with positive people who want the best for me.

69. I am a patient, calm and loving individual who is on the right path in life.

70. I live right here and now and accept the present moment.

71. I am grateful and joyful to live another day in this beautiful world.

72. I realize that I hold a tremendous amount of knowledge that can be used for good.

73. My experiences are unique to me and there's personal power in that.

74. I guide and help other gracious people with my experience and wisdom.

75. My uniqueness makes me uniquely successful.

76. I take one step at the time and always trust that I will reach my destination.

77. I am so happy and grateful for all the blessings in my life.

78. My being is overflowing with creative energy.

79. I am in perfect harmony with life.

80. I am at peace with who I am.

81. I am at peace with other people.

82. It's easy for me to live in abundance and prosperity.

83. I find it easy to be confident.

84. I greet the day with ease.

85. I praise people when they do something good that I honestly appreciate.

86. I praise and reward myself when I do something good.

87. I encourage others and always see the full potential of what they can be.

88. Every day, and in every way, I'm getting more and more confident.

89. I now realize the preciousness of life.

90. I attract happy and kind people into my life.

91. I am so grateful for the kindness of others.

92. I am so grateful for my strengths.

93. I make the right decisions with ease.

94. I am so happy and grateful now that I get to experience life with a positive mindset.

95. I am a master at creating long-lasting habits that have a positive impact on my life.

96. I radiate happiness, joy, confidence and graciousness.

97. Being and staying positive is easy for me.

98. I am open to the goodness of the Universe.

99. All my actions lead me to happiness and abundance.

100. I am so grateful for having all I need to be happy right now.

Conclusion

Affirmations lead our thoughts to a more powerful place. When you affirm good, you give yourself a break from the worry cycle that so many of us experience.

Remember that you shouldn't try to fight the ego when unpleasant thoughts arise. Instead, become aware and fully accept your thoughts. Say "oh, it's you again, hello" without judgement and you'll find that the thought loses its power. You are now beginning an unstoppable cycle where negative a thought no longer affects you and you're also constantly affirming the good.

If you have received any value from this second part of the book, would you be so kind to leave a review for the individual book?

Thanks for your support and I wish you a beautiful life filled with joy and abundance!

Part 3: Daily Affirmations

250 Positive Affirmations for Health, Wealth, Happiness and Love

Introduction

Affirmations are positive sentences or statements that are directed toward influencing our subconscious mind. Words and phrases you say in a loop, hold the power to involuntarily create mental imagines within the subconscious mind. They can inspire, motivate, drive, and energize you into manifesting or creating everything you desire. Repeating affirmations and the mental visuals that are created as a result of these repeated affirmations, has the power to affect our powerful subconscious forces, which in turn affects our actions, habits, thoughts, and feelings.

Just do the following small exercise if you are feeling a bit down or low. Say something positive such as,"I am a wonderful being of love, success, and happiness." Do this twenty times, at least thrice a day. Notice how you feel at the end of the day. Your thought frequency will almost always change from negative to positive!

The way it works has to do with our subconscious mind being unable to distinguish between reality and imagined reality. If you keep saying, "wealth, abundance, money, prosperity," etc., the subconscious mind doesn't know that you are actually aspiring toward wealth or abundance. It believes that you already have it, and directs your behavior in alignment with this thought, thus creating more wealth and abundance.

Unlike our conscious mind that knows the difference between reality and imagined reality, the subconscious mind believes what is fed into it as the truth. Using this powerful yet little-known principle of the subconscious mind, we can bring about a huge shift in our thought process automatically, to transform everything from our habits to our actions to our thought process. You can begin today—even if you think you have nothing or are nowhere near your goal.

I've been asked several times about what affirmations truly accomplish. To begin with, they keep you motivated to achieve your goal. Affirmations keep your mind firmly fixated on the goal. They affect the subconscious mind to activate its fulfillment powers. Affirmations possess the ability to impact the way you think and act when you communicate with people who have the ability to help you accomplish your goals.

Repeating positive statements in a loop makes you feel more energized, active, and positive, which in turn puts you in a better frame of mind to transform your external and internal reality. Thoughts indeed become things, and affirmations sow the seeds of positive thoughts in your subconscious mind.

Before beginning affirmations, ensure that you really desire to get what you are affirming. If there are doubts or you aren't sure about what you want, these uncertainties and doubts will get in the way. This is the primary reason people don't get results and end up losing their belief in the power of affirmations.

Say your affirmations with faith, interest, love, positivity, belief and feeling, if you truly want to change your thoughts or manifest your goals. You must say the affirmations with the belief that your wish or desire has already been fulfilled. This thought pattern will speed up the fulfillment of your affirmations!

The mind will occasionally throw up a few negative thoughts and doubts if your present reality is starkly different from what you want to accomplish. However, perseverance is the key to releasing negative thoughts and uncertainties that conquer you.

Chapter One: Affirmations for Wealth, Abundance and Prosperity

1. Wealth is showering and pouring into my life.

2. The Universe's riches are drawn to me easily and effortlessly.

3. I openly accept wealth, prosperity, and abundance now.

4. I am grateful for the overflowing, unrestrained, and limitless source of wealth.

5. Everything I turn my hand to returns riches and abundance.

6. I am a money magnet. Money is always attracted to me.

7. My life is completely filled with powerful and positive abundance.

8. All my needs are more than met.

9. I am prosperous and money gushes to me from multiple sources.

10. I am the fortunate receiver of wealth flowing from several revenue streams.

11. I give and receive graciously and I am a constantly flowing stream of wealth.

12. I graciously accept all the happiness, abundance, and wealth the Universe showers me with each day.

13. Income flows to me in unexpected ways.

14. I love money and money loves me.

15. All the money and wealth I want is flowing to me right now.

16. I am an overflowing treasure trove of abundance.

17. I easily, smoothly, and effortlessly attract financial prosperity, wealth, and abundance into each aspect of my life.

18. I always have more than enough money.

19. Money keeps flowing to me from expected and unexpected sources.

20. Money constantly circulates in my life freely and effortlessly.

21. There is always surplus money flowing to me.

22. I am financially free.

23. Money comes flying to me from several directions.

24. Money comes to me generously in perfect ways.

25. There is an abundance of things to love in my life and the lives of everyone around me.

26. I am perennially adding to income and wealth.

27. Money flows through me, and I have more than enough wealth to meet all my needs and wishes.

28. Money is flowing to me each day.

29. Money is drawn to me easily, effortlessly, and frequently.

30. I am a prosperity magnet. Prosperity and abundance is always drawn to me.

31. I think abundance all the time.

32. I am completely worthy of attracting wealth and money into my life.

33. I deserve wealth, money and abundance.

34. I am open and accepting to receive the wealth and abundance life has to offer me.

35. I embrace and celebrate new ways of generating income.

36. I draw, welcome, and invite unlimited sources of wealth, money, and income into my life.

37. I use money to better my own and other people's lives.

38. I am fully aligned with the energy of wealth and abundance.

39. My actions and deeds lead to continuous prosperity.

40. I attract money and wealth creation opportunities.

41. My finances are improving beyond my imagination.

42. Wealth is the root of comfort, joy, and security.

43. Money, spirituality, and contentment can completely coexist in harmony.

44. Money, love, and happiness can all be friends.

45. Money works for me.

46. I am the master of money, wealth, and abundance.

47. I am capable of handling huge sums of money.

48. I am completely at peace having a lot of money.

49. I can handle success with dignity and grace.

50. Wealth expands my life's experiences, passions, and opportunities.

51. Wealth creates a positive, fulfilling, and rewarding impact on my life.

52. I realize that money is important for leading a wonderful life.

53. The Universe is a constant provider of money and wealth for me, and I have more than enough wealth to meet all my needs.

54. My actions and activities make more money for me, and I am constantly supplied with money.

55. My bank balance increases each day, and I always have more than enough money and wealth for myself.

56. Wealth and I are buddies and we'll always be together.

57. Each day I attract and save more and more money.

58. Money is an integral aspect of my life and has never gone away from me.

59. I am free of debt, as money, wealth, and abundance are forever flowing in my life.

60. My money consciousness is forever increasing and has kept me surrounded by wealth, money, and abundance.

61. I have a highly positive wealth and money mindset.

62. I am highly focused on becoming wealthy, rich, and prosperous.

63. Attracting wealth, money, and abundance is easy.

64. My bank account value is growing by the day.

65. Money is wonderful energy.

66. My wealth and income automatically rise higher and higher.

Chapter Two: Affirmations for Love

67. I am totally worthy of love.

68. I am in love with myself for who and what I am.

69. I deserve unconditional love and happiness.

70. I am always surrounded by loving, caring and nurturing people in life.

71. I am responsible for my happiness and I love myself.

72. I am worthy of receiving a lot of love.

73. I've created a home filled with love, happiness, harmony, and joy.

74. The greater love I give, the more love I receive in return.

75. I am eternally grateful for every relationship and experience in my life.

76. I am a loving, giving, and forgiving person.

77. I treat the one I love with love, affection, and respect.

78. I am truly worthy of love and I deserve to be loved and respected.

79. I am in love with a person who adores me.

80. I love and accept other people as they are, which creates lasting relationships/friendships for me.

81. I am loved, desired, and cherished.

82. My relationships are filled with desire, love, passion, fun, care, and understanding.

83. I cherish all my emotions and feelings.

84. I attract the perfect partner who satisfies my needs in an inspiring and positive manner.

85. I am highly sensitive to the needs of other people I am surrounded by.

86. I am surrounded by love, respect, and gratitude.

87. I am in a loving, respectful, and passionate relationship.

88. I am loving and being loved all the time.

89. I am grateful for all the love enveloping my life.

90. I give and get love effortlessly and easily.

91. The person I love is with me always and the flow of love in our life only increases.

92. All the love I desire is within me.

93 I am loved and capable of giving love.

94. I am right now in a perfect relationship with a perfect partner.

95. I am surrounded by love all the time.

96. All my relationships are positive, caring, loving, inspiring and long-term.

97. I am truly worthy of being loved and deserve to receive love in absolute abundance.

98. I love everyone around me and others shower me with an abundance of love.

99. I always attract loving and caring people in life.

100. My partner and I are both in love and happy. Our relationship is truly glorious and joyous.

101. I attract loving, inspiring, caring, and positive people in my life.

102. I am thankful to the Universe for a loving and caring partner.

103. I have complete gratitude for attracting only healthy, loving, and positive relationships.

104. I am blessed to be with the love of my life. We treat each other with love, appreciation, and respect.

105. I happily attract and give love each day.

106. I am eternally grateful to my partner for how caring, positive, inspiring and nurturing they are.

107. Every day, I am grateful for being loved and for receiving the care that I do.

108. I completely trust that the Universe will bring me supporting, loving, caring, inspiring and positive relationships.

109. I open my heart to the knowledge that I deserve love.

110. Wherever I go and whoever I am with, I will always find love.

111. I totally deserve the love I receive, and I am open to the love the Universe bestows upon me.

112. I am attracted to love and romance, and love and romance are attracted to me.

113. I spread love and receive it several times over.

114. I trust the Universe will help me find my perfect soul mate.

115. I can feel and experience the love of those surrounding me immensely.

116. I love each and every aspect of my wonderful life.

117. Love fills my heart, body, and soul with warmth every day.

118. I become more loving, caring, and inspiring with each passing day.

119. Everything I do completely aligns with the vibration and frequency of love.

120. I give and receive love joyfully, amazingly, and freely.

121. My life is truly amazing because I find love everywhere I go.

122. I enjoy being with people who bring out the best in me.

123. I love being with folks who bring out my best side.

124. I see myself as a creature of love, happiness, passion, and joy.

125. I am loved and accepted. I am loved and accepted. I am loved and accepted.

126. I matter because I contribute love to this world in a wonderful and meaningful manner.

127. My partner and I are a true reflection of each other.

128. I create a sanctuary within my house that is forever inviting and welcoming to my partner.

129. I stand firm, strong, and grounded in my love.

130. Love originates from my core existence, and impacts all areas of my life.

131. I think positively and in a nurturing way about my partner.

132. I encourage my partner to aim for the stars.

133. My energy converts conflict into a sense of unity, alignment, and oneness.

134. I am content, happy, and joyful alone, and my partner just adds to the wonderful feeling that already exists.

135. I enjoy having fulfilling, rewarding, and nurturing relationships with my friends and family members.

136. I attract more, and appreciate the joy of giving and getting unconditional love.

137. I seek the love of my life, and the love of my life seeks me.

138. I am grateful for the romance and love that I am attracting in my life.

139. I speak, think, and behave from a place of love within me.

140. I spend time with a person who unconditionally accepts me as I am.

141. I wholeheartedly welcome the romance and passion gushing into my life.

142. My relationship grows stronger, more passionate, and romantic each day.

143. Emotional intimacy is an integral part of my relationship each day.

144. My relationship grows stronger each day, and my love grows much deeper.

145. I am blessed to be in love with a person who is my true soul mate.

Chapter Three: Affirmations for Health

146. I am fit, attractive, energetic, and healthy.

147. I am getting healthier, more energetic, and fitter every day.

148. I am stunning, inside out.

149. I care for myself by eating right, sleeping properly, and exercising.

150. I take longer, deeper, calm and relaxed breaths.

151. I love, care for and nurture my body, and it cares back for me.

152. I am very beautiful, fit, and attractive.

153. I am completely relaxed and filled with serenity and peace of mind.

154. I am in a relaxed state of mind.

155. My body heals, replenishes and repairs itself quickly.

156. I am beautiful in my body, mind and spirit.

157. I go to bed early, sleep deeply, and am an early riser.

158. I create healing energy throughout my life.

159. I am healthy, relaxed, and happy.

160. I am capable of manifesting maximum health and strength.

161. I am healthy,and confident, and physically and emotionally strong and happy.

162. I maintain my body weight effortlessly and easily at all times.

163. I am totally in control of my health, healing, and wellness.

164. I appreciate and adore my body, mind, and soul.

165. I have abundant and inexhaustible energy.

166. My skin is clear, glowing, and radiant.

167. I am capable of maintaining my perfect weight.

168. I am healthy in every aspect of existence.

169. I am an effective, healthy, fit, and energetic individual who is capable of handling anything that arises.

170. I will dedicate 15-20 minutes a day for exercising.

171. I feel vibrant, enthusiastic, and energetic every moment.

172. I enjoy eating nutritious, balanced, and healthy meals.

173. I have complete power to control my fitness and health.

174. I love to eat healthy food and exercise.

175. I am the recipient of glowing health and a vibrant mind, body, and spirit.

176. I am completely enjoying my daily exercise routine now.

177. I am fit, healthy, and active, and practice regular exercises.

178. My body is fit and healthy, and all my organs function perfectly well.

179. Each day, I get closer and closer to my perfect weight.

180. I eat to fuel and nourish my body when required.

181. I stay away from junk food. I eat healthy, nutritious, energy-giving, and balanced food that benefits my entire body.

182. I have a strong heart and a formidable steel body. I am healthy, vigorous, energetic, and filled with vitality.

183. With each passing day, my body gets healthier, more energetic, and stronger.

184. My body is a temple. It is holy, clean, and filled with a sense of goodness.

185. I breathe nice and deeply, exercise regularly, and feed my body nutritious food.

186. I am completely free from diabetes, high blood pressure, and any life-threatening disease.

187. I express my gratitude to God and everyone in my life.

188. I am healthy, wealthy, and wise. My body is healthy, my mind is wise, while I am always wealthy.

Chapter Four: Affirmations for Happiness

189. I am open to accepting new beginnings and journeys. I am learning, growing, and unlocking new and promising possibilities.

190. Every moment I appreciate the completeness of my journey, and I am aware that appreciating the completeness of my journey brings me greater happiness, peace, and joy for endless days.

191. The small joys add big happiness to my life when I become more mindful of their existence in my life.

192. I respect everything and everyone around me, and I perform even tiny actions with a lot of love, happiness, and gratitude.

193. I am strong, creative, and happy, and use my mistakes as stepping stones for growing into a wiser person.

194. I value inner peace and realize that being myself is completely acceptable. I live with my truth. Happiness is as much within us as outside of us.

195. I touch several lives. My happiness makes people around me happy and makes the world a huge, happy place.

196. I am truly grateful to the Universe for this wonderful and glorious life. I am truly grateful to everyone who has touched my life and has made it worth living.

197. Happy thoughts and circumstances are drawn to me naturally. I am forever landing in happy circumstances.

198. I am happy to perform random acts of compassion, kindness, love, and happiness. Love results in more love and happiness.

199. I am loving, happy, compassionate, and kind.

200. I am focused, enthusiastic, and excited to take on anything that comes my way, day in and day out, with a positive and energetic attitude.

201. I am truly grateful and appreciative for all that I possess, including love, happiness, compassion, and joy.

202. I feel a complete sense of joy, love, and happiness in the moment, and exude that energy throughout the day.

203. I feel gorgeous inside and out while defining my own sense of beauty through happiness, abundant love, and positive energy.

204. My abundance of love, positive energy, and happiness lets me step into the day to accomplish everything I can.

205. This day, I allow myself to experience the goodness that surrounds me, and retain a positive energy that flows throughout the day to nourish my body, mind, and spirit.

206. Happiness is my birthright. I choose to attract happiness, and I deserve to be truly happy and joyful in everything I do.

207. Today is a brand-new day that presents a new opportunity for starting afresh on a wonderful and positive note.

208. Today is the day for new beginnings, and I welcome the day with refreshed eyes and a rejuvenated mind.

209. Abundance is flowing throughout my day. I possess all the happiness, love, creativity, enthusiasm, and energy to make my day wow!

210. Each moment that I am alive, I become happier and happier.

211. Each living cell in my body is pulsating with joy, happiness, positivity, and abundance.

212. Each day that I am alive, I feel a great sense of joy, happiness, and positivity.

213. Each new day, I feel like I am having greater fun.

214. I feel like I am exploring and discovering new things that bring joy to me each day.

215. My happiness expands and soars each day.

216. Each day of my life is filled with a renewed sense of roses, rainbows, and sunshine.

217. Each day I welcome greater fun, joy, and happiness in my life.

218. I can't stop smiling because everything in my life feels right currently.

219. I think positive things, and am forever happy, peaceful, and joyous, irrespective of my external conditions.

220. Everything I come across throughout the day puts a smile on my face.

221. I often activate the feel-good chemicals in my brain to feel happy and smile a lot.

222. I decorate every day with laughter, joy, and cheer.

223. I let myself enjoy each moment of my day.

224. I always chase my bliss.

225. I always look for ways to attract more joy and laughter into my life.

226. I am complete within myself.

227. I am everything I choose to be.

228. I am healthy, happy, joyful, and strong.

229. Everything I need to be is within me.

230. I completely believe in myself and everything that I have to give the world.

231. I am bold, courageous, and brave.

232. I am free to create the life of my dreams and desires.

233. I am present, mindful, and aware.

234. The possibilities that life presents me with are infinite.

235. I am open to receiving.

236. I float happily and in a content manner within my world.

237. I deserve to be in a serene, calm, and peaceful state.

238. I choose to live a happy, balanced, and peaceful life.

239. I create a place of peace, tranquility and harmony for myself and others.

240. I find happiness, joy, and pleasure in the tiniest of things.

241. I can tap into my spring of internal happiness anytime I desire and let out a flow of joy, pleasure, happiness, and well-being.

242. I look at and observe the world with a smile, because I can't help but sense the joy around me.

243. I have great fun with even the most mundane of endeavors.

244. I have a wonderful sense of humor and love to share laughter and joy with others.

245. My heart is overflowing with a feeling of happiness and joy.

246. I rest in complete bliss and happiness each time I go to sleep, knowing only too well that everything is fine in my Universe.

247. Happiness is my right. I wholeheartedly embrace happiness as my state of being.

248. I am the most content and happiest person on this planet.

249. I am glad that all happiness originates from within me and I live every moment to the fullest.

250. I wake up every day with a joyful smile on my face and a sense of gratitude in my heart for all the wonderful moments that await me during the day.

Conclusion

I genuinely hope that this book was able to help you learn more about affirmations and offer practical strategies through which you can start using affirmations to transform your personal life more confidently. You will find several pointers on how to use affirmations in the right way to obtain optimum results.

The book is packed with plenty of affirmations for enjoying better health, wealth, love, and happiness. These affirmations are easy to remember and say and have the power to truly transform your life if used correctly.

The next step is to take action! A person who *does not* read is as good as a person who *cannot* read. Similarly, knowledge without action is pointless. One cannot transform one's life or use affirmations only by reading about them and feeling wonderful. You have to use certain pointers to make it work exactly the way you want, and most importantly, use affirmations consistently.

Affirmations work like a charm because they deeply embed a feeling frequency into the subconscious mind. If you repeat them, they influence the subconscious mind to act in a specific manner!

Lastly, if you enjoyed reading part 3, can you please take some time to share your views and post a review on the individual book?

Part 4: "I Am" Affirmations

250 Powerful Affirmations About Living in an Abundance of Wealth, Health, Love, Creativity, Self-Esteem, Joy, and Happiness

Introduction

The following chapters will discuss how to use affirmations to change your life in a positive direction. Many times, it can feel like you're surrounded by negative thoughts and feelings all day, every day. You feel like you've failed at life, work, and relationships. And the more you think about things in a negative way, the more negativity there is in your life.

It can be extremely hard to break the negative thinking cycle. Using positive affirmations can actually change how you think, and how you interact with the world around you. It's allowing yourself to get into a new habit, one that will change your life for the better. When used correctly, affirmations can effectively flip your view on things, and help you feel happier and healthier. They can help you to achieve success, both professionally and personally. You are able to learn to have love, joy, and happiness in your life, even if you haven't felt those emotions in a very long time. Affirmations can even help boost your self-esteem! They can do so much for you and improve your life in a way that nothing else can.

Think about it in a karma-type way. When we have a positive attitude and feel good about ourselves, our lives tend to run a lot more smoothly. It can be described as a sort of "vibration." When our vibration is positive, positive things like love, health, and wealth, are magnetically drawn to us. The opposite can also be true. When we have a negative attitude and feel bad about ourselves, we might harbor a self-defeating type of behavior. Doing so causes negative outcomes, like illness, drama, and financial woes. Instead of focusing on all the negative aspects of our lives, we can use affirmations to help us look at all the positivity that surrounds us. We're able to focus our attention toward goals, both long-term short-term, step away from stress, and promote self-change in a positive manner.

There are plenty of books on this subject on the market; thanks again for choosing this one! Every effort was made to ensure it is full of as much useful information as possible. Please enjoy!

Chapter 1: Wealth

1. I deserve money. I attract large amounts of money to me. I deserve to have lots of money.
2. I am great at managing my money. I am the master of my money. I am in control of my finances.
3. I am grateful for the wealth in my life at this moment. I am grateful for the wealth already inside of me.
4. I am rich. I am a rich woman/man. I attract wealth from all around me.
5. I give value to others. I create value for others. I am a being full of unlimited creative ideas and thoughts.
6. I bless all those who are rich, abundant, and wealthy. I bless their abundance and wealth and send my love their way.
7. I am becoming wealthier and wealthier every day, in every way.
8. I am becoming more abundant every day, in every way.
9. I am becoming richer and richer every day, in every way.
10. I use money for good things. Money is good because I use it for good.
11. I become richer by giving more. I become wealthier by giving more. I become abundant by giving more.
12. I am a millionaire. I think like a millionaire, I act like millionaire, and I feel like a millionaire.
13. I allow wealth to come into my life. I allow prosperity to come into my life. I allow abundance to come into my life.
14. I am receptive to all the wealth that life offers me.
15. My success is important and necessary.
16. My dreams have come true.
17. Every day is a wealthy day.
18. I create wealth, so I am always wealthy.
19. I am positive toward being wealthy.
20. I welcome wealth with open arms.
21. I expect success in all my endeavors and allow success to be my natural state.
22. I make setbacks and mistakes my stepping stones to my success.
23. I am able to move past challenges quickly.

24. I am able to move from a poverty mindset to an abundance mindset.
25. Money comes to me in an easy and effortless way.
26. I align myself with the energy of wealth and abundance.
27. I embrace new income opportunities.
28. I use my money to better my life and the lives of those around me.
29. I am capable of handling large quantities of money.
30. Money creates a positive impact on my life.
31. I handle success with grace.
32. I am the master over my wealth.
33. I am able to receive money.
34. I allow my wealth to expand, and live in comfort and joy.
35. I am able to make money doing what I love and am fully supported in my ventures.
36. I think positive money thoughts.

Chapter 2: Health

1. I eat healthy food that benefits my body.
2. I drink large quantities of water which cleanses my body.
3. I feel good, my body feels good, and I radiate good feelings.
4. I am in possession of a healthy mind and a healthy body.
5. I have a strong heart and healthy body. I am energetic and vigorous.
6. I let go of all bad feelings within me about others, incidents, and everything else. I forgive everyone who is associated with me.
7. I treat my body as a temple. My body is clean, holy, and full of goodness.
8. My body is healthy, I am wealthy, and my mind is wise.
9. I surround myself with people who encourage me to be healthy.
10. I honor my body.
11. I am looking forward to a healthy old age because I take care of my body now.
12. I am grateful for my healthy body.
13. Peace flows through my mind, body, and soul.
14. I enjoy living life.
15. I am worthy of good health.
16. I focus on positive progression.
17. I am a friend to my body.
18. I look after my body with unconditional compassion.
19. I am doing everything possible to keep my body well.
20. I am willing to participate in my wellness plan.
21. I have a strong immune system. I am able to deal with germs, bacteria, and viruses.
22. My body is full of energy.
23. My body is free from pain.
24. My body heals itself, and I feel better every day.
25. I send lots of love and healing to all my organs.
26. I pay attention to my body. I listen to what my body needs.
27. I am a good sleeper. I sleep soundly and wake up feeling rested.
28. I surround myself with people who support my healthy choices.

29. I speak, think, and act in perfect health.
30. I choose to make all my thoughts healthy ones.
31. I enjoy taking care of my body.
32. I breathe deeply to lift my mood and bring energy to my body.
33. I allow all the cells in my body to repair and replenish it.
34. I nourish my body with lots of water.
35. I have fun when exercising my body.
36. I listen to my body, which communicates what it likes to me.

Chapter 3: Love

1. I am surrounded by love.
2. I keep my heart open.
3. I radiate love.
4. I deserve to love and be loved in return.
5. I always get what I give out into the world.
6. I am able to see from my partner's point of view, so I am able to understand my partner perfectly.
7. I am able to express my feelings openly.
8. All of my relationships offer a positive and loving experience.
9. I am happy to give and receive love every day.
10. I am grateful for how loved I am, and how much people care about me.
11. I have the power to give love endlessly.
12. I welcome love with open arms.
13. I allow my inner beauty to radiate outward.
14. My relationships fulfill me.
15. I am beautiful.
16. I trust in the universe to find me my perfect match.
17. I feel love. I see love. I am loved.
18. I love myself and every aspect of my life.
19. I look at everything with loving eyes, and I love everything I see.
20. My partner loves me for who I am.
21. I respect and admire my partner.
22. I see the best in my partner.
23. I share emotional intimacy with those I have a strong relationship with.
24. My partner and I communicate openly.
25. I am able to resolve conflicts with my loved ones in a peaceful and respectful manner.
26. I am able to be myself in a romantic relationship.

27. I support my partner and want the best for him/her.
28. I deserve compassion, empathy, and love.
29. I have a caring and warm heart.
30. I am filled with love for who I am.
31. My life is filled with love.
32. Love flows through me in every situation.
33. I find love wherever I go.
34. I am able to receive love with open arms.
35. I am supported by my family, friends, relationships, and I love it.

Chapter 4: Creativity

1. I make time to create.
2. I constantly develop as an artist.
3. I let my creative self out to play.
4. I give myself room for creative expression.
5. I am creative.
6. I have a free and open mind.
7. I have an active and free imagination.
8. I am full of creativity and inspiration.
9. My creative mind is the best resource for overcoming challenges.
10. I am open to new experiences.
11. I make nurturing my mind a priority.
12. I embrace and love my creative inner child.
13. I am my unique self. I am special, wonderful, and creative. I direct my creative talents toward anything that gives me pleasure.
14. I use my creativity in every aspect of my life.
15. My gifts are appreciated by those around me, and my talents are wanted.
16. I can create miracles within my life.
17. I let go of all resistance when expressing my creativity.
18. There is a lot of opportunity in whichever creative area I choose.
19. Even if unsuccessful, all my creative ventures bring me satisfaction.
20. I am open to learning new creative ideas every day.
21. I practice being creative every day, and it is a top priority in my life.
22. I become more creative every day.
23. I am able to solve problems using creative and unique ideas.
24. I am full of creativity.
25. I have power and resources as a creator.
26. I am a powerful, creative being with unlimited ideas.
27. I am capable of thinking up new and fresh ideas.
28. I am grateful that I have an imaginative mind.

29. I am grateful for all of my different creative ideas.
30. I am grateful for my creative abilities.
31. I am imaginative.
32. I am resourceful and inventive.
33. I am always able to count on my imagination for inventive ideas.
34. I use my power and gifts in helpful and inspiring ways.
35. I am able to feel creative and inspired when I am at work.
36. I have a fantastic creative talent.

Chapter 5: Self-Esteem

1. I am willing to accept mistakes. They are the stepping stones to success.
2. I am always learning and growing.
3. I will not compare myself to others.
4. I focus on the things I can change.
5. I deserve a good life. I toss away the ideas of suffering and misery.
6. I love myself as I am.
7. I am constantly growing and changing for the better.
8. I am smart, competent, and able.
9. I believe in myself, in my skills, and in my abilities.
10. I am useful and make contributions to society and my own life.
11. My decisions are sound and reasonable, and I stand by them.
12. I have the capability to acquire all the knowledge I need to succeed.
13. I am free to make my own decisions and choices.
14. I am worthy of others' respect.
15. I accept compliments easily and give them freely.
16. I accept other people as they are, which in turn allows them to accept me as I am.
17. I respect myself.
18. I let go of the need to prove myself to others. I am my own self, and I love me as I am.
19. I am full of courage. I am willing to act despite fear.
20. I trust myself.
21. I approach strangers with enthusiasm and boldness.
22. I breathe in a manner that helps me to feel more confident. I inhale confidence and exhale timidity.
23. I am confident of my future.
24. I am a self-reliant, persistent, and creative person in everything I do.
25. I make confidence my second nature.
26. I am able to find the best solution to my problems.
27. I remember that nothing is impossible.
28. I am unique. I feel good. I love living life and being me.

29. I have integrity.
30. I accept myself fully.
31. I am proud of myself.
32. I allow my mind to fill up with nourishing and positive thoughts.
33. I accept myself and find inner peace in doing so.
34. I have the ability to overcome all challenges that life gives me.
35. I am capable of rising up in the face of adversity.
36. I make my own decisions and choices.

Chapter 6: Joy

1. I am willing to allow joy in my life.
2. I show joy to all that I interact with.
3. I choose joy. It is a possibility in each and every moment of my life.
4. My day begins and ends with joy and gratitude for myself.
5. My experiences in joy expand every day.
6. I let myself feel appreciation and joy for the people who love me.
7. I give myself permission to feel joy.
8. I allow myself to be open to experiencing more joyous moments every day.
9. My words, actions, and thoughts support my joyful living.
10. I choose joy to be a part of my inner self.
11. I am happy with all of my achievements.
12. I make choices and decisions that nurture me and bring me joy.
13. I greet every day with gratitude and joy.
14. I am allowed to feel joy.
15. I let myself concentrate on thoughts that make me happy.
16. I give joy away to others so I can receive it in return.
17. I understand that it is okay to feel joy when others do not.
18. Experiencing life brings me great joy.
19. One joyful experience opens up the door to many more joyful experiences.
20. I allow my joy to empower me to new heights.
21. I smile and feel joy at the world around me.
22. Even the simple things in life allow me to feel joy.
23. I feel joy in being alive.
24. I am able to find joy in the simple things.
25. I love to share my joy with others.
26. I am able to find joy in every moment that happens.
27. I welcome joy into my life.

28. I am able to accept joy and peace in all aspects of my life.
29. I let go of all anxiety, worry, fear, and doubt, and fill myself with peace, love, and joy.
30. I create a home full of joy.
31. I do my best every day, which fills me with joy.
32. I share freely the joy I feel in my heart.
33. I enjoy doing nice things for other people.
34. My everyday responsibilities give my life balance and joy.
35. I am able to make whatever I am doing enjoyable.

Chapter 7: Happiness

1. I am happier than I have ever been.
2. I understand that it is okay to be happy.
3. I choose to be happy.
4. I deserve to be happy.
5. I share my happy thoughts and experiences with others.
6. Happiness is something that's contagious. I understand this and spread happiness around to others, which in turn brings it back to me.
7. My happiness helps the people around me to feel happy.
8. My happy attitude attracts other happiness into my life.
9. I am grateful for my wonderful life. I am grateful to everyone who has made me happy and made my life worth living.
10. I am happy when I make progress toward my goals.
11. I focus more on my present happiness than my past mistakes.
12. I see happiness wherever I go.
13. I can pick myself up and lift my own spirits.
14. I feel a sense of happiness and peace within myself.
15. I am a positive person and choose to have a positive view.
16. I have all that I need to be happy.
17. I am ready to tackle whatever comes my way with a positive and happy attitude.
18. I am happy. I am healthy. I am strong.
19. Happiness is my birthright. Happiness is my natural state of being.
20. I wake up every morning feeling happy about life.
21. I approach life with a sense of humor and love to laugh with others.
22. My life brightens and lightens when I think happy thoughts.
23. Although I am working hard on my goals, I remember that it's important to have fun.
24. Being happy is a top priority in my life, and I remember to practice this feeling every day.
25. I allow myself to enjoy the little moments I observe every day around me.
26. I am always on the lookout for ways to bring more happiness and laughter into my life.
27. I am always able to find a reason to smile.

28. I am happy with the choices I make in life.
29. I am friendly with other people and smile at them.
30. I spread happiness everywhere I go.
31. I commit myself to developing the highest possible level of happiness in my life.
32. I bring happy thoughts with me everywhere I go.
33. I love my happy memories and think of them often.
34. I practice laughing each day.
35. I enjoy laughing. I laugh as often as I can.
36. I am happy and free, and exactly as I was born to be.

Conclusion

Thanks for making it through to the end of *"I Am" Affirmations: 250 Powerful Affirmations About Living in an Abundance of Wealth, Health, Love, Creativity, Self-Esteem, Joy, and Happiness.* I hope it was informative and able to provide you with all of the tools you need to achieve your goals.

The next step is to actually use these affirmations in your normal day-to-day routine. Maybe you're suffering from depression, or just unhappy with how your life is going. Maybe you're having a hard time at your job, or really want to make some big changes in your life. Using affirmations is a great first step toward making these changes! The biggest roadblock is you, and your way of thinking. For example, it is all too easy to tell yourself that you're not going to work out because you're not good at it. Using affirmations can turn that kind of thinking completely around, and help you become a much healthier person.

To sum it up, affirmations are these amazing positive statements that help you challenge and overcome negative and self-sabotaging thoughts. It might seem really silly to tell yourself that you feel pretty every day. But think about it like this - we do repetitive exercises for our physical health, don't we? Some of us go running; some of us go to the gym and lift weights. There are many different sorts of physical exercises, but they all have the same thing in common. And that's that they help us to improve our physical health. So why should our mental and emotional health be any different?

Finally, if you found part 4 useful in any way, a review on Amazon for the individual book is always appreciated!

Part 5: Affirmations for Success

250 Positive Affirmations for Creating Powerful Daily Habits to Start the Morning with Self-confidence, Make Money and Build Beneficial Relationships

Introduction

Affirmations are positive, inspiring and motivating statements that can be said aloud or silently to yourself. By repeating these statements, you are affirming it loud and clear to your subconscious mind to influence your actions.

Let's say you have an important job interview coming up. You keep affirming to yourself that you have "a wonderful interview." The subconscious mind believes this to be true because it can't distinguish between what you want and your reality. When the subconscious mind believes this statement to be true, it directs all your actions toward having an amazing job interview, thus actually helping you pass the interview with flying colors.

Our subconscious mind has the power to shape our reality. By repeating positive statements over and over, we embed them in our subconscious which acts upon them to create the reality we desire.

Affirmations are for your mind what physical exercise is for the body. Continual repetition of these positive statements helps reprogram our subconscious mind for success. It helps eliminate self-limiting beliefs and negative feelings to transform a person from his or her limited thinking and mediocre thoughts.

The power of affirmation bestows upon your reality endless possibilities. "I cannot" becomes "I definitely can," and renewed self-confidence replaces your fears and insecurities. Affirmations are reminders for your subconscious mind to stay on track. They keep you focused on your goals, and help you come up with effective solutions for roadblocks and challenges along the way.

Your thoughts have a powerful frequency that has the potential to create your reality. Affirmations create stronger vibrations for joy, success, love, health, and appreciation. Through the law of attraction, these positive statements attract people, opportunities, and things to help you accomplish your innermost desires. Knowingly or otherwise, we use affirmations. However, we are likely not doing it right, which means we are not attracting what we want to bring into our lives. By constantly talking or thinking about things we do not want, we only create more of them!

Reciting affirmations daily, interrupts and replaces our negative thoughts, ideas and beliefs. To accomplish this, you must continually flood the subconscious mind with visuals of the brand-new reality you desire to create.

The most important thing to ask yourself is whether you really want what you are affirming. Doubts and uncertainties will stand between you and your goals. Also, you must believe you truly deserve what you want to accomplish. If your belief loses its power, affirmations may fall flat. The reason people are not able to get results is that they do not believe in their goals or do not think they deserve to accomplish these goals.

Affirm with complete faith, love, passion, and interest. Believe and act as if your desire has already been fulfilled. These positive thoughts speed up your thinking toward fulfilling the goal faster and more effectively. Of course, when your current circumstances and your goals are very far apart, it is natural to have negative thoughts. However; perseverance is the key.

Chapter One: Affirmations for Self-Confidence

1. I deserve to be happy, fulfilled and successful.

2. I hold the power and potential to change myself.

3. I can make my own choices and decisions.

4. I am free to make my own choices and decisions.

5. I can choose to live as I want while giving priority to my desires, goals, and dreams.

6. I pick happiness each time I want, irrespective of the circumstances.

7. I am open, adaptive, and flexible to change in each sphere of my life.

8. I operate from a position of confidence, self-assuredness, and high self-esteem each day of my life.

9. I always do my best.

10. I am deserving of the love I receive.

11. I like meeting strangers and approaching them with enthusiasm, interest and boldness.

12. I am creative, perseverant and self-reliant in everything I do.

13. I appreciate change and quickly adapt myself to new circumstances.

14. I always observe the positive in others.

15. I am one of a kind. I feel wonderful about being alive, being happy, and being me.

16. Life is rewarding, fun, and enjoyable.

17. There are a lot of awesome opportunities for me in all aspects of life.

18. My life is full of opportunities everywhere.

19. Challenges always bring out the best in me.

20. I replace "must," "should," and "have to" with "choose," and notice the difference.

21. I choose to be in a state of happiness right now. I enjoy my life.

22. I appreciate all that is happening in my life now. I really love my life.

23. I live in a place of joy.

24. I am brave, courageous, and fearless.

25. I am positive, optimistic, and always believe that things will turn out best.

26. It is easy for me to make friends as I attract positive, compassionate and kind people into my life.

27. I am a powerful creator because I make the life I desire.

28. I am alright because I love and accept myself as I am.

29. I completely trust myself, and I am a confident person.

30. I am successful in my life right now.

31. I am passionate, enthusiastic and inspiring.

32. I have peace, serenity, calmness, and positivity.

33. I am optimistic that everything will work out only for the best.

34. I have unlimited resources, power, confidence, and positivity at my disposal.

35. I am kind, loving, and compassionate, and care about others

36. I am persistent, perseverant, and focused. I never quit.

37. Self-confidence is my second skin. I am energetic, passionate and enthusiastic.

38. I treat everyone with kindness, compassion, and respect.

39. I inhale self-confidence and exhale doubts.

40. I am flexible and adapt to change instantly.

41. I possess endless reserves of integrity. I am reliable and do exactly what I say I will.

42. I am smart and intelligent.

43. I am competent and capable.

44. I completely believe in myself.

45. I recognize and identify all the good qualities I possess.

46. I am fabulous, glorious, and awesome. There's no one else like me.

47. I always see the best in everyone around me.

48. I surround my life with people who bring out the best in me.

49. I release negative thoughts and feelings I have about myself.

50. I love the person I become each day.

51. I am forever growing, nurturing, and developing.

52. My opinions match who I truly am.

53. I deserve all the happiness and success in the world.

54. I possess the power to change myself.

55. I am competent in making my own choices and decisions.

56. I have complete freedom to choose to live the way I want, and give priority to my desires and wishes.

57. I choose happiness each day, irrespective of my external circumstances.

58. I can confidently speak my mind.

59. I have respect for others, which makes others like and respect me in return.

60. My thoughts, opinions, and actions are invaluable.

61. I am confident that I can accomplish everything I want today and every day.

62. I have something wonderful and special to offer the world.

63. People love, admire, and respect me.

64. I am an amazing person who feels great about myself and my wonderful life.

65. I am doing the best I am able to with the experience, skills, and knowledge I have.

66. Feeling great about myself is second nature to me.

67. I have dedication, discipline, and good habits.

68. I always keep my promises, which makes people love and respect me.

69. I treat myself with kindness and compassion.

Chapter Two: Affirmations for Success

70. I have the power, potential, and ability to create all the prosperity, success, and abundance I desire.

71. My mind is completely free of resistance and is open to new, exciting, and wonderful possibilities.

72. I deserve to be successful and am worthy of receiving all the good that life has to offer me.

73. I am thankful for all the talents, abilities, and skills that contribute to my success.

74. The Universe is filled with unlimited opportunities and possibilities for my career.

75. I am open-minded and eager when it comes to exploring new avenues and possibilities for success.

76. I recognize every opportunity that knocks on my door and seize it immediately.

77. Each day I discover exciting, promising, and interesting new paths to travel.

78. I see and experience prosperity everywhere I look.

79. I love my work. It is rewarding, fulfilling, gratifying, and a part of my journey toward greater success.

80. My ambition is in perfect harmony with my personal and professional values.

81. I work with inspiring, passionate, enthusiastic, and fascinating people who share my zest for work and success.

82. By creating success for myself, I am also creating opportunities for the success of others.

83. I feel powerful, positive, confident, and calm as I take on new challenges.

84. I attract successful and powerful people who motivate, understand, and inspire me.

85. I celebrate every goal I achieve with happiness and thankfulness.

86. The more successful I get, the more confident and powerful I feel.

87. I forever attract the perfect circumstances at the perfect time. I am in the right place at the right time.

88. I am grateful for all the success flowing into my life.

89. I totally trust my intuition to guide me toward making smart and wise decisions.

90. I keep focused on my vision and pursue my everyday work with zeal and passion.

91. Each day is filled with new possibilities, ideas, and avenues that inspire me.

92. Success comes easily and effortlessly to me because I excel in everything I do.

93. I take complete pride in my ability to make worthy contributions to the world around me.

94. I always expect positive results, and as a result, I naturally attract them.

95. I am fortunate to attract brilliant and powerful mentors who generously share their knowledge, wisdom, and ideas with me.

96. As I allow abundance and success in my life, even more doors to success and opportunity open up for me.

97. I set very high standards for myself and always live up to them.

98. I have an inexhaustible supply of brilliant new ideas that help me become more successful with each passing day.

99. I am constantly creating a life of happiness, success, and abundance.

100. I love the person I am, and I invariably attract people who admire and respect me as a unique person.

101. I am making the planet a better place to live by being a powerful, inspiring, and positive influence.

102. I think and dream big, which always brings me success.

103. Each day I dress up for success, abundance, and prosperity in mind, body, and spirit.

104. I am truly grateful for my success, abundance, and financial prosperity.

105. I am enthusiastic and passionate about being more successful.

106. The Universe is somehow always helping me accomplish my goals and desires.

107. My dreams become manifest right before my eyes.

108. The Universe's wealth is forever circulating within my life, and flowing to me in avalanches of success and prosperity.

109. I am ambitious, driven, inspired, and motivated by my goals each day.

110. I have the power to lift myself and my spirits up whenever I desire.

111. I find it easy and effortless to be optimistic.

112. Success is naturally and effortlessly drawn to me in all areas of my life.

113. My affirmations for happiness, prosperity, and success always bear results.

114. Other people are driven and motivated by my success.

115. I am decisive in my actions which lead to greater success, happiness, and prosperity.

116. It is easy for me to accomplish all my goals.

117. The Universe is my buddy and helps me accomplish all my desires, dreams, and goals with ease.

118. Other people are attracted to me because I am forever successful.

119. I am forever enhancing all aspects of my life.

120. I have the desire and willpower to climb great heights of success.

121. I offer myself wholeheartedly to the Universe, and it showers me with unlimited rewards and success.

122. The vision I have creates success that surrounds me.

123. Happiness, joy, success, and prosperity are second nature to me.

124. Accomplishing my goals is so easy and effortless.

125. I am continuously enhancing all areas of my life.

126. I am where I desire to be right now.

127. My life is an incredibly amazing, exciting, and wonderful journey.

128. My beliefs and thoughts create my reality, and I am the master of my thoughts.

129. I have the power to create my life exactly the way I desire.

130. Everything I deeply desire, need, and want is already out there waiting for me to

come and get it.

131. I am full of endless positive energy, positive thoughts, and positive actions.

132. I am destined for success and greatness.

133. Today and every day, I take several steps toward the fulfillment of my goals.

134. My mind, positive energy, tenacity, and ability can move mountains.

135. I feel refreshed, determined, driven, and excited to excel today and each day.

136. My thoughts, ideas, and beliefs are the seeds for success.

Chapter Three: Affirmations for Wealth, Prosperity and Abundance

137. My actions create consistent wealth, abundance, security, and prosperity.

138. I am fully aligned with the energy of money, wealth and abundance.

139. I am open, accepting, and receptive to all the wealth that the Universe has to offer.

140. Unimaginable wealth and abundance are always drawn to me.

141. I always allow myself to be drenched in financial abundance, and I generously share it.

142. Money and riches flow through me like never-ending ocean waves.

143. I am always thinking of money, wealth, prosperity, and abundance.

144. I am a wealthy and rich entrepreneur who is living a dream life on my own terms.

145. I radiate the aura of wealth, prosperity, riches and abundance.

146. My riches are always growing as I offer more of myself to serve the world.

147. I am financially prosperous, and money comes to me naturally and abundantly.

148. I let myself be drenched with prosperity, abundance, wealth, and financial success.

149. Riches always find their way to me, and they keep coming back.

150. Money is wonderful. I love and adore money.

151. I have all the money and material resources in the world to provide me with everything I desire.

152. Each day, more and more money is drawn to me at the speed of light.

153. Earning money through multiple sources comes easily and effortlessly to me.

154. Money is free-flowing energy that naturally and effortlessly comes into my life all the time.

155. My energies are aligned to receive money, abundance, and prosperity from the Universe.

156. There is no limit to the amount of wealth, prosperity, money, and abundance that I am capable of making.

157. I am very wealthy, prosperous, and rich. Money flows to me from all directions.

158. I pursue all my dreams to obtain wealth, and enjoy everything I desire in life.

159. I am grateful for the money, abundance, and wealth that enters my life all the time.

160. I invest 100% of my energy in large deals that earn me a lot of money.

161 When I receive great wealth, I realize that it is a direct result of the service I give to other people.

162. I feel fulfilled, blessed, and happy that I am able to provide generously for my loved ones.

163. There is no limit to the amount of wealth, assets, and money I can own.

164. I am grateful that I have more money, wealth, prosperity, and abundance than I ever imagined.

165. I am happy, blessed, and grateful because I always have more than enough of everything I desire and need.

166. I am in deep gratitude to divine providence for the magnificent flow of great and endless abundance in every aspect of my life.

167. I am deeply prosperous, and grateful for everything that the Universe has to offer.

168. Prosperity and abundance are attracted to me all the time, and I am in turn attracted to them.

169. I am extremely happy now, because positive and amazing things continue to happen in my life.

170. I have a very grateful heart that keeps drawing everything I desire toward me.

171. I realize I totally deserve to be prosperous, rich, and wealthy in all that I do.

172. My gratitude increases with every good thing that enters my life as a blessing from the Universe.

173. The world is indeed a wonderful place to live in, and I am enjoying my positive and enthusiastic journey here.

174. I am forever surrounded by joy, happiness, and love wherever I go.

175. I am a creative, innovative, inspiring, and prosperous being.

176. I keep creating new and wonderful, positive habits that take me closer to my goals and help me build wealth and prosperity.

177. I begin each day with a deep sense of gratitude, positive energy, and excitement and joy for all the abundance that awaits me.

178. I am very happy because I have everything I want. I love myself and everyone around me.

179. I am in a constant state of joy, prosperity, abundance, and fulfillment. I am free to do what I desire.

180. I have unlimited and inexhaustible resources to enjoy the life of my dreams and desires.

181. My work is an all-consuming affair that helps me attract everything I need and want.

182. I am eternally grateful to the Universe for the wealth, prosperity, and abundance in my life.

183. I am a part of the infinite Universe, where I am deeply connected with everything I need, now and in the future.

184. I am invaluable to other people, and they are invaluable to me. I am a being of limitless creative ideas, actions, and thoughts.

185. There is more than enough wealth and abundance for everyone. There is abundance, wealth, money, and prosperity everywhere I go.

186. Being wealthy and rich is my birthright. I deserve to be rich, as it is a part of my identity. Rich is what I am.

187. I bless all the prosperous, abundant, rich and wealthy people. I bless their riches and wealth and send them great love.

188. I am a child of God, the Universe, and the higher self. I can have everything I see around me.

189. I become richer each day through multiple sources of wealth.

190. Money is great because I use it for wonderful things. I use wealth for the highest good for everyone.

191. Money is energy that is created in the mind. Money is in my mind. My mind and thoughts create money for me continuously, day after day.

192. I deserve to have plenty of money. I attract huge amounts of money all the time wherever I go.

193. Being rich, wealthy, and prosperous gives me the power to touch the lives of countless people while making a huge difference in their lives. Money and abundance allow me to help people.

194. I am a wonderful money manager and the master of my destiny. I am completely in control of my wealth and financial life.

195. Every penny that flows into my life works hard for me and helps me create more and more wealth each day.

196. The more money I give, the richer, wealthier, and more prosperous I become.

197. My loved ones benefit from my wealth, prosperity, and abundance. They are truly grateful for the riches and wealth that are within me.

198. I am eternally grateful for the abundance I enjoy in my life right now.

199. I wholeheartedly embrace every positive association with money, abundance, Wealth, and prosperity.

200. I breathe wealth and abundance. Each breath I take increases the sense of abundance, prosperity, and awareness surrounding me.

201. I have a millionaire mindset. I think, act, feel, and behave like a true millionaire. I am a millionaire.

202. I let wealth, abundance, and prosperity flow freely into my life.

Chapter Four: Affirmations for Beneficial Relationships

203. I am willing to look at situations in different ways by being open to the ideas and input of others around me.

204. I forgive others and let go, knowing that I am forgiven too.

205. I bring positivity to each day, knowing well that it will be multiplied in other people around me.

206. I see other people as the Universe's blessing to me.

207. I choose to see and believe in the goodness of everyone around me.

208. I always look for the best in everyone.

209. I am always open and ready to serve others, because service is integral to true leadership.

210. People are a blessing meant to nurture and enrich my world.

211. I am always surrounded by love, and everything around me is fine.

212. I make my partner feel loved and appreciated every single day. We both are each other's support system.

213. I know I am wonderful and I deserve love.

214. The more I invest in myself, the better my relationships will be.

215. I am always attracting loving and caring people in my life.

216. An inexhaustible stream of love originates from my being.

217. An endless and infinite stream of love, joy, and happiness radiates from within me.

218. I have limitless love, joy, and friendship to offer people.

219. The more love I give, the more I am capable of receiving.

220. The Universe guides me and positively influences me in all my relationships.

221. All my relationships are loving and harmonious.

222. My Universe is overflowing with positive and loving relationships.

223. I am a manifestation of divine love.

224. I am guided by the unconditional love of the Universe.

225. My relationships always work out for the greatest good of everyone.

226. The door to great, unconditional, and inexhaustible love is always open to me.

227. The Universe has loving relationships set up for me. I am ready to enjoy them.

228. I enjoy being the best version of myself for my and my partner's happiness.

229. I trust my partner more and more each day.

230. I enjoy being in a rewarding and fulfilling relationship.

231. My partner's happiness and joy matter to me.

232. There is deep trust and understanding between my partner and me.

233. Each day of my life is filled with endless love.

234. My partner is attracted to every bit of me and finds me sexy.

235. I always use loving, soulful, and kind words while communicating with people.

236. I have found my soul mate, since I am a loving and compassionate person who deserves true love.

237. I communicate with my partner in a kind, gentle and loving manner.

238. All my relationships are healthy because they are deeply rooted in love, joy, and compassion.

239. Forgiveness, love, and compassion form the basis of all my relationships.

240. I exude love and positivity, and others give love right back to me.

241 My life is filled with love, and I find love everywhere I go.

242. My partner is physically, mentally, and spiritually drawn to me.

245. My romantic relationships are healthy, fulfilling, and long-lasting.

246. My partner is an attractive, passionate, and charming person. We share great sexual chemistry.

247. My partner and I are divinely matched as soul mates.

248. I celebrate my love and life each day.

249. Magic, love, and miracles surround my relationships

250. I deserve a person who is loyal and faithful to me.

Conclusion

I sincerely hope it was able to help you learn more about success, wealth, relationship and other affirmations, while also providing practical strategies through which you can start using affirmations for transforming your personal life.

This book is packed with plenty of affirmations to attract better health, wealth, love, and success. These affirmations are easy to remember and say, and have the power to truly change your life if used correctly.

74552933R00057

Made in the USA
Columbia, SC
13 September 2019